Rose

by Iain Gray

WRITING to REMEMBER

79 Main Street, Newtongrange,
Midlothian EH22 4NA
Tel: 0131 344 0414
E-mail: info@lang-syne.co.uk
www.langsyneshop.co.uk

Design by Dorothy Meikle
Printed by Blissetts
© Lang Syne Publishers Ltd 2025

All rights reserved. No part of this publication may be reproduced, stored or introduced into a retrieval system, or transmitted in any form or by any means (electronic, mechanical, photocopying, recording or otherwise) without the prior written permission of Lang Syne Publishers Ltd.

ISBN 978-1-85217-774-4

Rose

MOTTO:
Constant and true

CREST:
A harp upon a chapeau

TERRITORY:
Nairn

NAME variations include:
Roos
Roose
Ròs *(Gaelic)*
Ròis *(Gaelic)*

Chapter one:

The origins of popular surnames

by George Forbes and Iain Gray

If you don't know where you came from, you won't know where you're going **is a frequently quoted observation and one that has a particular resonance today when there has been a marked upsurge in interest in genealogy, with increasing numbers of people curious to trace their family roots.**

Main sources for genealogical research include census returns and official records of births, marriages and deaths – and the key to unlocking the detail they contain is obviously a family surname, one that has been 'inherited' and passed from generation to generation.

No matter our station in life, we all have a surname – but it was not until about the middle of the fourteenth century that the practice of being identified by a particular surname became commonly established throughout the British Isles.

Previous to this, it was normal for a person to be identified through the use of only a forename.

But as population gradually increased and there were many more people with the same forename, surnames were adopted to distinguish one person, or community, from another.

Many common English surnames are patronymic in origin, meaning they stem from the forename of one's father – with 'Johnson,' for example, indicating 'son of John.'

It was the Normans, in the wake of their eleventh century conquest of Anglo-Saxon England, a pivotal moment in the nation's history, who first brought surnames into usage – although it was a gradual process.

For the Normans, these were names initially based on the title of their estates, local villages and chateaux in France to distinguish and identify these landholdings.

Such grand descriptions also helped enhance the prestige of these warlords and generally glorify their lofty positions high above the humble serfs slaving away below in the pecking order who had only single names, often with Biblical connotations as in Pierre and Jacques.

The only descriptive distinctions among the peasantry concerned their occupations, like 'Pierre the swineherd' or 'Jacques the ferryman.'

Roots of surnames that came into usage in England not only included Norman-French, but also Old French, Old Norse, Old English, Middle English, German, Latin, Greek, Hebrew and the Gaelic languages of the Celts.

The Normans themselves were originally Vikings, or 'Northmen', who raided, colonised and eventually settled down around the French coastline.

They had sailed up the Seine in their longboats in 900AD under their ferocious leader Rollo and ruled the roost in north eastern France before sailing over to conquer England in 1066 under Duke William of Normandy – better known to posterity as William the Conqueror, or King William I of England.

Granted lands in the newly-conquered England, some of their descendants later acquired territories in Wales, Scotland and Ireland – taking not only their own surnames, but also the practice of adopting a surname, with them.

But it was in England where Norman rule and custom first impacted, particularly in relation to the adoption of surnames.

This is reflected in the famous *Domesday Book*, a massive survey of much of England and Wales, ordered by William I, to determine who owned what, what it was worth and therefore how much they were liable to pay in taxes to the voracious Royal Exchequer.

Completed in 1086 and now held in the National Archives in Kew, London, 'Domesday' was an Old English word meaning 'Day of Judgement.'

This was because, in the words of one contemporary chronicler, "its decisions, like those of the Last Judgement, are unalterable."

It had been a requirement of all those English landholders – from the richest to the poorest – that they identify themselves for the purposes of the survey and for future reference by means of a surname.

This is why the *Domesday Book*, although written in Latin as was the practice for several centuries with both civic and ecclesiastical records, is an invaluable source for the early appearance of a wide range of English surnames.

Several of these names were coined in connection with occupations.

These include Baker and Smith, while Cooks, Chamberlains, Constables and Porters were to be found carrying out duties in large medieval households.

The church's influence can be found in names such as Bishop, Friar and Monk while the popular name of Bennett derives from the late fifth to mid-sixth century Saint Benedict, founder of the Benedictine order of monks.

The early medical profession is represented by Barber, while businessmen produced names that include Merchant and Sellers.

Down at the village watermill, the names that cropped up included Millar/Miller, Walker and Fuller, while other self-explanatory trades included Cooper, Tailor, Mason and Wright.

Even the scenery was utilised as in Moor, Hill, Wood and Forrest – while the hunt and the chase supplied names that include Hunter, Falconer, Fowler and Fox.

Colours are also a source of popular surnames, as in Black, Brown, Gray/Grey, Green and White, and would have denoted the colour of the clothing the person habitually wore or, apart from the obvious exception of 'Green', one's hair colouring or even complexion.

The surname Red developed into Reid, while

Blue was rare and no-one wanted to be associated with yellow.

Rather self-important individuals took surnames that include Goodman and Wiseman, while physical attributes crept into surnames such as Small and Little.

Many families proudly boast the heraldic device known as a Coat of Arms.

The central motif of the Coat of Arms would originally have been what was sometimes borne on the shield of a warrior to distinguish himself from others on the battlefield.

As highlighted on page three, a feature of some Coats of Arms are the clan or family motto and crest – with the latter on occasion different from the central motif'.

Adding further variety to the rich cultural heritage that is represented by surnames is the appearance in recent times in lists of the most common names found throughout the United Kingdom of ones that include Khan, Patel and Singh – names that have proud roots in the vast sub-continent of India.

Echoes of a far distant past can still be found in our surnames and they can be borne with pride in commemoration of our forebears.

Chapter two:

Norman roots

Ranked 69th in some lists of the 100 most common surnames found in the United Kingdom today, bearers of the Rose name can trace a descent back through the dim mists of time to 1066.

This was when King Harold II, the last of the Anglo-Saxon kings, was defeated and killed at the battle of Hastings in October of that year by Duke William of Normandy.

Declared King William I of England in December, the complete subjugation of his subjects followed.

Those Normans who had fought on his behalf were rewarded with the lands of Anglo-Saxons, many of whom sought exile abroad as mercenaries while, within an astonishingly short space of time, Norman manners, customs and law were imposed.

The Rose name derives from the lordship of Ros, near Caen, in Normandy and it was a knight of this lordship who accompanied William on his conquest and was subsequently rewarded with the grant of lands in Kent.

In common with many other Norman families – more properly by this time known as Anglo-Normans – a branch of the Ros, or Rose, family was later granted lands in Scotland during the reign from 1124 to 1153 of King David I.

He had spent some time in captivity in England but, despite this, had become enamoured with Anglo-Norman customs and manners.

Accordingly, he invited some to settle in Scotland – granting them lands in the full knowledge that to protect and retain them they would serve his own interests by helping to uphold the authority of the Crown through quelling 'rebellious' native Scots.

One Rose family was given lands in Nairn, in the northeast of the kingdom, and it was through the marriage in about 1290 of a Hugo de Ros of Geddes to Marie de Bosco, heiress of another Anglo-Norman family awarded lands in Nairn and who was also related to the family of de Bisset, or Bisset, that the Roses acquired the lands of Kilravock.

Their seat eventually became Kilravock Castle, on the banks of the River Nairn.

Built in about 1460, the castle has been run by the Kilravock Castle Trust since 1984 and serves as a popular conference centre.

In 2013, meanwhile, The Lord Lyon King of Arms of Scotland officially recognised David Rose as 26th Baron of Kilravock and Chief of Clan Rose.

One of a dynasty of distinguished bearers of the Rose name, Sir John Rose was the Scots-born lawyer and politician created 1st Baronet Rose of Montreal.

Born in 1820 at Gask, near Turriff, Aberdeenshire, his father William Rose was a great-grandson of Hugh Rose, the 16th Laird of Kilravock and Chief of Clan Rose who died in 1755.

Educated at King's College, Aberdeen, Sir John Rose was aged sixteen when he travelled with his British Army officer father to Huntingdon, Quebec, in what was then Lower Canada.

Staying there, he studied law and was admitted to the bar in 1842 and subsequently set up a legal practice in Montreal.

Combining his legal skills with politics, he served from 1857 to 1867 as a member of the Legislative Assembly of the Province of Canada and later in high level government posts that included Solicitor General for Canada, Minister of Finance and Minister for Public Works.

A delegate on behalf of Canada to the

Colonial Conference in London in both 1867 and 1868, he moved to England in 1869 and, in addition to practicing law, held government posts that included Privy Counsellor and Receiver General of the Duchy of Cornwall.

Created 1st Baron Rose of Montreal in 1872, he died in 1888, while he was the father of Sir William Rose, 2nd Baronet of Montreal and Sir Charles Day Rose, 1st Baronet Rose of Hardwick House.

Sir William Rose, who inherited his father's baronetcy on his death, was born in Montreal in 1846.

Spending most of his life in England and a partner in a stock brokerage firm, he was the owner of the 60-acre Moor Park estate at Farnham, Surrey.

He died in 1902, while his younger brother Sir Charles Day Rose, born in Montreal in 1847, was not only a British-Canadian businessman and Liberal Party politician, but also a noted racehorse breeder, yachtsman and aviator.

Based at Newmarket, Suffolk, and a member of the Jockey Club, he bred famous racehorses that included Isinglass and Cyllene.

A Thoroughbred racehorse and sire, Isinglass won eleven races between 1892 and 1895, including the Epsom Derby in 1893, the 2000 Guineas at Newmarket and the St Leger Stakes at Doncaster.

Also a Thoroughbred and sire, Cyllene won major races between 1897 and 1899 and sired four Epsom Derby winners.

A competitive yachtsman, Rose was a member of the exclusive Royal Victoria Yacht Club.

Elected Liberal MP (Member of Parliament) for Newmarket in a 1903 by-election, he was elevated to the Peerage six years later as 1st Baronet Rose of Hardwick House – the house being the property he had previously bought in Whitchurch, Oxfordshire.

We do not know if Rose was flattered or not, but parts of Hardwick House were used by E.H. Shepherd for his illustrations for Kenneth Grahame's popular children's book *The Wind in the Willows* – and Rose himself is thought to have been one of the models for "Toad" of Toad Hall.

Also a keen aviator and president for a time of the Royal Aero Club, he died after suffering a heart attack in 1913 while travelling back by car to Hardwick House from Hendon Aerodrome.

Chapter three:

Battle honours

Bearers of the Rose name have also gained distinction on the bloody field of battle.

One noted nineteenth century military commander and diplomat was Field Marshal Sir Hugh Henry Rose, 1st Baron Strathnairn and whose family had connections to the Roses of Kilravock.

Born in 1801 in Christchurch, Hampshire, his father was Sir George Rose of Sandhills, in Christchurch, who served as British Minister Plenipotentiary at the Prussian court.

Educated by officers of the Prussian Army, Sir Hugh returned to British shores where, in 1820, he was commissioned in the 93rd Sutherland Highlanders.

His subsequent military career saw him rise rapidly through the ranks and his involvement in some of the greatest conflicts of his age.

His first posting was to Ireland, where he joined the 19th Regiment of Foot, then involved in attempting to quell agrarian unrest against landlords.

By 1829, with the rank of captain, he had joined the 93rd Highlanders as a company commander and, a year later, was appointed equerry to the Duke of Cambridge.

His first foreign posting saw him serving in Gibraltar and Malta with the 92nd Highlanders while in 1840, with the rank of colonel, he served as a military adviser in Syria to the Ottoman Army during the Egyptian-Ottoman War.

Appointed British consul-general for Syria and Lebanon in 1841, at a time when there was almost genocidal warfare between the rival Druze and Maronite sects, he was responsible for the daring rescue of 700 American missionaries, who had been caught up in the conflict, from Mount Lebanon.

Rose took charge of leading them to the safety of Beirut – insisting on walking all the way on foot in order that his horse should be available to carry old women.

Transferring to the diplomatic service in 1848, he was appointed chargé d'affairs three years later at the British Embassy in the Turkish capital of Constantinople, and was closely involved in the diplomatic crisis that eventually led to the Crimean War of 1853 to 1856.

A conflict between Russia and Turkey and the latter's allies that included France and Britain, it was sparked off by Russian demands that they be allowed to give 'protection' to all Orthodox Christians in Turkey – in effect an attempt to encroach on aspects of Turkish sovereignty.

Attached to the headquarters of the French Army during the war, on one occasion Rose was personally responsible for putting out a fire that had threatened to blow up an ammunition store.

This would have had devastating consequences, and the French gratefully awarded him the Legion of Honour.

Fighting with the French regiment the 1st Zouaves, he was wounded at the battle of Alma in September of 1854 and again at the battle of Mamelon in June of the following year.

By 1857, the much travelled soldier and diplomat was in India.

This was during the Indian Rebellion against British rule and, among other daring actions, Rose managed to re-take a number of forts that the rebels had captured.

Appointed Commander-in-Chief, India in 1860, he returned to Britain five years later and was named Commander-in-Chief of British forces in Ireland.

Raised to the Peerage as Baron Strathnairn in 1866 and, a year later, to the rank of general, he died in 1885 – eight years after having been promoted to field marshal.

The highest ranking American to be killed in action in Europe during the Second World War and, at the time of his death, the highest ranking person of the Jewish faith to serve in the U.S. Army, Major General Maurice Rose was born in 1899 in Denver, Colorado.

The son and grandson of rabbis originally from Poland, he served during the First World War with the 89th Infantry Division, while during the Second World War he served with the 1st Armored Division, 2nd Armored Division and the 3rd Armored Division.

Promoted to the rank of major general in August of 1944 he was given command of the 3rd Armored Division that, known as the "Spearhead", was the first to penetrate the formidable German defences known as the Siegfried Line.

He was killed in March of 1945 near Paderborn after the jeep in which he was travelling suddenly encountered a group of German Tiger tanks.

The jeep was surrounded, and the true nature of what subsequently transpired remains unclear.

A tank crew member approached the jeep and shot the major general several times as he reached towards his pistol holster – in all probability to throw his weapon to the ground as a sign of surrender, knowing resistance would be futile.

Whether or not the German soldier thought Rose was intending to open fire or, indeed, surrender – the consequence was that up to 110 German prisoners-of-war are claimed by some sources to have been shot in reprisal by furious U.S. troops.

Described by his biographers as "Word War II's Greatest Forgotten Commander", his many honours and awards include two Oak Leaf Clusters, Legion of Merit, the Distinguished Service Cross and the Distinguished Service Medal while the Rose Medical Center in his home city of Denver is named in his honour.

Bearers of the Rose name have also excelled in the highly competitive world of business.

Born in 1949 in Gosport, Hampshire, Stuart Rose, more formally known as Baron Rose of Monewden, has held a number of executive positions that include with the Burton Group,

Argos, Booker plc, the Arcadia Group and Marks and Spencer.

Chief executive of the latter from May of 2004 to May of 2010 and now an independent non-executive director of the company, he was elevated to the Peerage as Baron Rose of Monewden, in the County of Suffolk, in 2008.

Chief executive of Rolls-Royce plc from 1996 to 2011, Sir John Rose is the British businessman born in 1952 in Blantyre, Malawi.

Having had a banking career at a senior level with Security Pacific and First National Bank of Chicago and executive positions with other companies that include the Rothschild Group and the Aerospace Group, he was knighted in 2003.

One bearer of the Rose name with a rather unusual claim to fame was the early twentieth century New York underworld figure Jack Rose.

Born Jacob Rosenzweig in Poland in 1876 and immigrating to the United States with his family at an early age, he went on to run a number of gambling clubs in New York that included the notorious East Side Manhattan Club, *The Rosebud*.

The club became a hang-out for a number of underworld figures and other shady characters, and police tried to close it in 1912. But it was allowed to remain open – after Rose agreed to pay the head of the police 'Gambling Squad', 25% of the club's weekly take.

Also implicated in the murder of the gambler Herman Rosenthal, Rose escaped prosecution after acting as a star witness against others involved.

He died in 1947 – having renounced gambling and warning of its evils – while his legacy lives on in the form of the classic cocktail *Jack Rose*.

Particularly popular in the 1920s and 1930s, and named after Rose because of his own popularity at the time, it consists of grenadine, applejack, and lime or lemon juice.

Chapter four:

On the world stage

A leading English actor of stage and film, George Rose was born in Bristol in 1920.

The son of a butcher, he studied at the Central School of Drama, London and, after military service during the Second World War, made his West End debut in 1946.

On Broadway, his credits include the 1964 production of *Hamlet*, the 1965 *Royal Hunt of the Sun* and the 1968 *Loot*, while he received a Tony Award nomination for his performance in the 1969 musical *Coco* and another Tony nomination and a Drama Desk Award for Outstanding Performance for his role in the 1974 comedy *My Fat Friend*.

His performance in a Broadway revival of *My Fair Lady* netted him a number of awards that include a 1976 Tony Award for Best Actor in a Musical and a similar award for the 1986 production *The Mystery of Edwin Drood*.

With film credits that include the 1952 *The Pickwick Papers*, the 1958 *A Night to Remember*, *The Pirates of Penzance*, from 1983, and television credits that include the mini-series *Holocaust* and *Naked City*, he died in 1988.

Born in 1951 in Lynwood, California, **Cristine Rose** is the American actress whose many credits include the television remake of the 1986 film *Ferris Bueller's Day Off*, co-starring with Jennifer Aniston, *Ally McBeal*, *Murder, She Wrote* and *Star Trek: The Next Generation*.

She is also noted for her role from 2006 to 2010 of Angela Petrelli in the series *Heroes*.

Named a Disney legend in 2011 following her starring roles in the 2006 *Dreamgirls* and the 2009 animated film *The Princess and the Frog*, **Anika Rose** is the American stage and screen actress and singer born in 1972 in Bloomfield, Connecticut.

Winner of a Tony Award for Best Featured Actress in a Musical for her performance in the 2004 *Caroline, or Change*, she was also nominated for a Tony for Best Featured Actress in a Play for the 2014 Broadway revival of *Raisin in the Sun*.

Behind the camera lens, **Jack Rose** was the screenwriter born in 1911 in Warsaw – then part of the Russian Empire – and who later immigrated to the United States.

Starting as a gag writer for comedians who

included Bob Hope and Milton Berle, his later screenwriting credits include the 1943 *Road to Rio*, starring Hope and Bing Crosby.

Nominated three times for Academy screenplay awards – for the 1955 *The Seven Little Foys*, the 1958 *Houseboat* and, from 1973, *A Touch of Class*, he died in 1995.

A noted contemporary English film director, **Bernard Rose** was born in London in 1960.

The winner when he was aged 15 of a BBC amateur film competition, he went on to work for Jim Henson's *The Muppet Show* and also on his 1981 film *The Dark Crystal*.

Graduating a year later from the National Film and Television School with a Master's in Filmmaking, he directed the controversial video for the 1983 Frankie Goes to Hollywood chart hit *Relax*.

Best known for his work on the 1992 horror cult classic *Candyman*, his other major credits include the 1994 *Immortal Beloved* – about composer Ludwig van Beethoven, and which he also wrote – the 1997 *Anna Karenina*, the 2013 *Boxing Day* and, from 2015, *Frankenstein*.

Born in Manhattan in 1920, **Reginald Rose** was a pioneering American television and film writer.

Much of his early work focussed on political and social issues and in 1954 he wrote *Twelve Angry Men* – concerning a jury deciding on the fate of a teenager accused of murder – and which was first screened as a television drama.

Receiving an Emmy Award for his work on the teleplay, he received an Academy nomination in 1957 for his film adaptation, starring Henry Fonda.

The creator and writer of the courtroom drama *The Defenders*, which won two Emmy Awards for Dramatic Writing, his big screen credits include the 1956 *Crime in the Streets* and, in a different genre, the 1978 *The Wild Geese* and the 1982 *Who Dares Wins*. He died in 2002.

Another award-winning American screenwriter, **William Rose**, was born in St Louis, Missouri, in 1918.

Travelling to Canada at the outbreak of the Second World War in 1939, before America had entered the conflict, he volunteered to fight overseas.

Settling in England for a time after the war, he went on to write a number of British comedy films that most notably include *Genevieve*, from 1953, before working in the land of his birth on films that include the 1954 *The Maggie*, the 1955 *The*

Ladykillers and the 1967 *Guess Who's Coming to Dinner* – for which he won an Academy Award for Writing, Screenplay.

Winner of the Writers Guild of America Award for Best Written American Comedy for the 1966 *The Russians are Coming, The Russians are Coming*, he was presented in 1973 with the guild's Laurel Award for Screenwriting.

The screenwriter, who had a brief romantic relationship with the actress Katharine Hepburn, died in 2002.

Born in Boston in 1915, **Kay Rose** was the American sound editor who won an Academy Award for Sound Editing for her work on the 1984 film *The River* – the first female to do so.

With other credits that include the 1947 *Mr Ashton was Indiscreet*, the 1958 *The Fantastic Disappearing Man* and the 2001 *Donnie Darko*, she received an Academy Special Achievement Award in 1985.

Also the recipient of a Motion Picture Sound Editors Lifetime Achievement award, she died in 2002.

Born in 1924 in Swanage, Dorset, **David E. Rose** is the retired British television producer and commissioning editor who was the producer from 1962 to 1965 of the police series *Z-Cars*, in addition to its spin-off *Softly, Softly*.

Also responsible for producing works for the BBC by playwrights including Willy Russell, Alan Bleasdale, Mike Leigh and David Hare, he was appointed Channel 4's commissioning editor for fiction in 1981.

Particularly identified with the channel's *Film on Four* enterprise, his many credits include, in 1985, *My Beautiful Laundrette*, *Dance with a Stranger* and *Letter to Brezhnev* and the 1986 *Mona Lisa*.

Recipient of a special prize for services to cinema at the 1987 Cannes Film Festival, he was awarded a British Film Institute (BFI) Fellowship in 2010.

Bearers of the Rose name have also excelled in the highly competitive world of sport.

On the high seas, one intrepid bearer of the name was the English sailor Sir Alec Rose who, in 1967-1968 single-handedly circumnavigated the globe.

Born in Canterbury in 1908, he served in the Royal Navy during the Second World War and, after the conflict ended, he learned to sail in what had been a lifeboat before buying the 36-foot cutter *Lively Lady*.

Having converted it to a ketch by adding a mizzenmast, he sailed her in the 1964 transatlantic race, finishing in fourth place.

Meanwhile, taking 226 days – from August 27, 1966 to May 28, 1967 – fellow English sailor Sir Francis Chichester became the first person to sail single-handedly around the world by what is known as the clipper route, and achieving the fastest navigation.

Rose, who along with his wife Dorothy ran a greengrocer shop in Southsea, had already been planning his own attempt at circumnavigation.

Although he did not match Chichester's time for the feat, what he did accomplish with *Lively Lady* was no less impressive.

Leaving Portsmouth on July 16, 1967 and, having had at one stage to make for Bluff Harbour, New Zealand, to repair a damaged mast, he eventually made landfall 354 days later – on July 10, 1968 – at Southsea.

His circumnavigation had ended only ten days before his 60th birthday, and he was later knighted in addition to being made a Freeman of the City of Portsmouth.

He later became a highly popular author, with books that include his account of the voyage, *My Lively Lady*, and *My Favourite Tales of the Sea*.

Admiral of the Ocean Cruising Club, he was described by Tim Heywood, a founder member of the club, as "the epitome of the breed of great seamen: quiet, reserved and humble."

He died in 1991, and a plaque commemorating his achievement is sited near the spot where he made landfall at Southsea, while he is also remembered through the RNSA (Royal Naval Sailing Association) Sir Alec Rose Trophy for Outstanding Single Handed Achievement.

Lively Lady, meanwhile, survives as a seaworthy vessel and is used by a charity for training in sail.

On the golf course, **Justin Rose**, born to English parents in Johannesburg, South Africa, in 1980 and moving to England when he was aged five, is the leading player who won the 2013 U.S. Open and the men's individual tournament at the 2016 Olympics.

Tying for fourth place as an amateur at the 1998 British Open Championship, winner of the 2007 Order of Merit on the European Tour and the 2012 World Golf Championship, he climbed to No. 1 in the

Official World Golf Ranking in 2018, a year after being made MBE for services to golf.

From golf to the rough and tumble of rugby, **David M. Rose** is the Scottish former rugby league player who won caps playing for both Scotland and Great Britain.

Born in 1931 in Jedburgh, in the Scottish Borders and a member of the Great Britain team that defeated France in the final of the 1954 Rugby League World Cup, he played at club level for Jed-Forest and English team Leeds.

In the world of the written word, **Karen Rose**, born in 1964, is the best-selling American romantic suspense novelist whose works include the trilogy *Die for Me*, *Scream for Me* and *Kill for Me*.

From the written word to art, **Christopher Rose** is the British wildlife artist born in 1959 in Kilembe, Uganda.

A member of the Society of Wildlife Artists (SWLA) and a recipient of the 1991 and 2001 European Bird Artist of the Year Award, his books include the 2005 *In a Natural Light*.

In the world of music, **Felipe Rose** is one of the founder members of the American disco group the Village People.

Born in 1954 in New York City to a Lakota Sioux father and a Puerto Rican mother, his band – with Rose dressed in 'Red Indian' attire – was formed in 1977 and has had international hits that include the 1978 *Macho Man* and, in the same year, the disco favourite *Y.M.C.A*.

As a solo artist, Rose's 2000 single *Trails of Tears* was nominated for three Nammy (Native American Music) Awards, while Village People are actively involved in a number of charities that include the Native American College Fund and AIDS charities.

Lead vocalist of the American heavy rock band Guns N' Roses, **Axl Rose** was born in 1962 in Lafayette, Indiana.

Formed in Los Angeles in 1985 and featuring the lead guitarist known as 'Slash', the band enjoyed chart success until the original line-up split up in 1994 with albums that include their 1987 *Appetite for Destruction* – one of the best-selling debut albums of all time.

In a decidedly different musical genre, **David Rose**, born in London in 1910 and immigrating as a child to the United States, was the songwriter, composer and pianist best known for his 1958 *The Stripper*.

It has been featured in a number of films, including the 1997 *The Full Monty*, while Rose was also responsible for other popular compositions that include *Calypso Melody* and *Holiday for Strings*.

Also having written the themes for a number of television series that include *Bonanza*, *Highway Patrol* and *Little House on the Prairie* and a recipient of a star on the Hollywood Walk of Fame, he died in 1990.